CHASE NORDMAN

# Talk Like a Teacher

*Real Responses to the Real Things Students Say*

Copyright © 2025 by Chase Nordman

All rights reserved. No part of this publication may be reproduced, stored or transmitted in any form or by any means, electronic, mechanical, photocopying, recording, scanning, or otherwise without written permission from the publisher. It is illegal to copy this book, post it to a website, or distribute it by any other means without permission.

First edition

This book was professionally typeset on Reedsy.
Find out more at reedsy.com

# Contents

*Why this book exists*   x
*How to use this book*   xii

I   Pushback, Refusal, and Limits

| | |
|---|---:|
| "This is boring/I am bored." | 3 |
| "I don't get this." | 4 |
| "I already know this." | 5 |
| "I don't want to." | 6 |
| "You can't make me." | 7 |
| "I don't care." | 8 |
| "Why do we have to learn this?" | 9 |
| "This is stupid." | 10 |
| "I'm not doing this." | 11 |
| "Can I just do it later?/I'll do it later." | 12 |
| "I did it in my head." | 13 |
| "Is this for a grade?" | 14 |
| "Can I just guess?" | 15 |
| "Nobody else has to do this." | 16 |
| "Why are you calling on me?" | 17 |
| "I'm not good at this." | 18 |
| "I give up." | 19 |
| "I'm done." (When they're not) | 20 |
| "I can't do this." | 21 |
| "I'm scared I'll mess up." | 22 |

| | |
|---|---|
| "I'm trying but I just don't get it." | 23 |
| "I hate this class." | 24 |
| "I hate this school." | 25 |
| "I hate you." | 26 |
| "You do too much." | 27 |
| "You're not funny." | 28 |
| "You never said that." | 29 |
| "You aren't my mom/dad." | 30 |
| "You're a bad teacher." | 31 |
| "This _____ is trash." | 32 |
| "This is torture." | 33 |
| "Leave me alone." | 34 |
| "I don't even respect my mom." | 35 |
| "Whatever." | 36 |
| "Shut up." | 37 |

## II   Identity and Insecurity

| | |
|---|---|
| "I'm fat." | 41 |
| "I want to be skinny." | 42 |
| "I'm ugly." | 43 |
| "I don't like how I look." | 44 |
| "I want plastic surgery one day." | 45 |
| "I'm gay." | 46 |
| "I'm trans." | 47 |
| "I feel invisible." | 48 |
| "I wish I wasn't here." | 49 |
| "I suck." | 50 |

III  Peer Drama and Conflict

| | |
|---|---|
| "I don't want to be their friend anymore." | 53 |
| "My classmate is so annoying." | 54 |
| "I'm not saying sorry." | 55 |
| "Shut up." (to a peer) | 56 |
| "You just called him/her_____" | 57 |
| "They keep touching my hair." | 58 |
| "I am being bullied." | 59 |
| "I'm always in trouble." | 60 |
| "Nobody wants to go with me." | 61 |
| "I don't have anyone to sit with." | 62 |
| "Nobody likes me." | 63 |

IV  Grief, Home, and Big Reveals

| | |
|---|---|
| "My mom/dad died." | 67 |
| "My sibling died." | 68 |
| "My grandparent died." | 69 |
| "My pet died." | 70 |
| "I'm being abused." | 71 |
| "Another student touched me inappropriately." | 72 |
| "An adult touched me inappropriately." | 73 |
| "My family doesn't like/want me." | 74 |
| "I want to run away." | 75 |
| "My parents are getting a divorce." | 76 |
| "My parent is going to jail." | 77 |
| "I'm moving." | 78 |
| "I'm pregnant." | 79 |
| "I feel hopeless." | 80 |
| "I feel depressed." | 81 |

"I want to kill myself." 82

## V  Authority and School

"My parents say it's OK to hit back." 85
"My mom said she's going to get you fired." 86
"Do you believe in God/Are you a Christian?" 87
"You're picking on me." 88
"You're mean." 89
"You're racist." 90
"I don't trust teachers." 91
"That's not how another teacher does it." 92
"I hate (other teacher)." 93
"Can I stay in your room this period?" 94
"Can I eat lunch with you?" (And you have to say 'no') 95
"Why do we have to write an essay?" 96
"I'm not a good test taker." 97
"This is too much work!" 98
"I'm not good at (subject)." 99
"I hate reading." (If they cannot read) 100
"I hate reading." (If they can read) 101
"Can I just use the internet?" 102
"I don't want to say the Pledge of Allegiance." 103
"I wasn't listening/I didn't hear you." 104
"I don't have a pencil." 105
"That's not fair." (Social) 106
"That's not fair." (Academic) 107
"Why did I get a (grade)? 108
"What can I do to improve my grade?" 109
"I don't want/need to graduate." 110
"This doesn't matter to me." 111

"School is pointless." 112
"What's the point?" 113

## VI  Body Needs and Embarrassing Moments

"I'm having a bad morning/day." 117
"I'm (too) tired." 118
"I'm hungry/Do you have food?" 119
"I'm sleepy (after lunch)." 120
"My classmate smells bad." 121
"I have to throw up." 122
"I just threw up." 123
"I just peed/soiled myself." 124
"I just started my period." 125
"Everyone's staring at me." 126

## VII  Restoration, Repair, and Trust-Building

"I'm sorry." 129
"I love you." 130
"You're my favorite teacher." 131
"Why do you keep trying with me?" 132

## VIII  Pocket Phrases

When a student gets off topic 135
When an inappropriate sexual topic comes up 136
When a slur is used 137
When a student is crying (uncontrollably) 138
When you want to shut down a behavior gently 139
When you remind them of your expectations 140

| | |
|---|---|
| When you want to acknowledge effort | 141 |
| When you need to pause to gather yourself | 142 |
| When you want to calm a tense moment: | 143 |
| When you want to redirect without power struggle: | 144 |
| When you want to connect after conflict: | 145 |
| When you want to encourage a fresh start | 146 |

## IX    Student Archetypes

| | |
|---|---|
| The Little Dynamo | 149 |
| The Sensitive Soul | 150 |
| The Big Feelings/Small Kid | 151 |
| The Anxious Test-Taker | 152 |
| The Class Clown | 153 |
| The Quiet Observer | 154 |
| The Perfectionist | 155 |
| The Screen Teen | 156 |
| The Activist | 157 |
| The Shut Down Student | 158 |

## X    Grade-Specific Responses

| | |
|---|---|
| Kindergarten | 161 |
| First Grade | 162 |
| Second Grade | 163 |
| Third Grade | 164 |
| Fourth Grade | 165 |
| Fifth Grade | 166 |
| Sixth Grade | 167 |
| Seventh Grade | 168 |
| Eighth Grade | 169 |

Ninth Grade . . . . . . . . . . . . . . . . . . . . . . . . 170
Tenth Grade . . . . . . . . . . . . . . . . . . . . . . . . 171
Eleventh Grade . . . . . . . . . . . . . . . . . . . . . . 172
Twelfth Grade . . . . . . . . . . . . . . . . . . . . . . . 173

## XI  Power Phrases

List . . . . . . . . . . . . . . . . . . . . . . . . . . . . . . 177

## XII  Final words and Acknowledgments

Talk Like a Teacher . . . . . . . . . . . . . . . . . . . 181

*About the Author* . . . . . . . . . . . . . . . . . . . . 183

# Why this book exists

I created *Talk Like a Teacher* because I kept having the same thought over and over again:

**"I wish someone would just tell me what to say."**

Not during the lesson plan but during the *moments*. The moments that punch through your routine and objectives and leave you blinking at a student who just said:

"I hate this class."

"I want to run away."

"Do you believe in God?"

"I think I'm pregnant."

I wrote this because I've been that teacher, standing in the overcrowded hallway, in the chaos of the last period of the day, knowing that how I respond in the next five seconds could either build trust or do serious damage. And I know I am not alone.

*Talk Like a Teacher* isn't a script.

It's more of a quick reference survival kit.

A confidence boost.

A map that you keep in your glove compartment for when the road takes a turn you didn't expect.

This book is filled with real things students actually say: raw, funny, painful, bold, and sometimes completely out of nowhere. And for each one, I offer a clear, calm, relational response plus an explanation of **why it works**. Because tone matters. Timing matters. The student and you matter. So does how you communicate.

This is for the teacher who wants to respond, not react.

For the para, the principal, the substitute, the counselor or anyone standing in the face of student emotion and looking for the words that lead to somewhere better.

I made this because I believe teaching is not just instruction, it's a conversation. And every tough moment is really a chance to show a student:

**"You can bring all of who you are here and I won't back away. I will be here."**

You don't need the perfect response to every situation.

You just need to *Talk Like a Teacher.*

# How to use this book

Each page in *Talk Like a Teacher* is headed with a real **student statement**: something blunt, surprising, defiant, emotional, or just human. Below that, you will find a response (**You say**) crafted to be trauma-informed, emotionally safe, and rooted in best practice *not* reaction. Then comes the **Why it works** breakdown, so you can understand the reasoning behind the words and make it your own.

This book is **not a script.**

Here's how to get the most out of it:

**Use it as a guide, not a gospel.**

If a phrase doesn't sound like you, tweak it. Subtract, add, or swap out language to fit your voice or your students. What matters most is that you do protect the **spirit** of the response to:

Avoid escalation

Avoid power struggles

Avoid language or tones that harm identity, dignity, or trust

**Keep it trauma-informed and with students at the center.**

These responses are designed with student nervous systems in mind. They prioritize calm over control, safety over sarcasm, connection over correction. Keep that lens as you adapt them because not every student needs the same tone or pace.

**Use it before the moments, during the moments, and after the moments.**

You can flip to a page during your prep, screenshot for a tough meeting, or sit down with it after a hard day to think:

"What could I have said differently?"

This book grows with you.

**Share it. Discuss it. Push back on it.**

Use pages from the book in staff meetings, PDs, or coplanning sessions. Build your school's culture of response together! Highlight parts you love. *Cross out what doesn't land.* Argue about tone. That's the work!

**Keep it close.**

On your desk. In your bag. In the notes or photos app of your phone. You'll be surprised how often a student will throw you a curveball that already lives in these pages.

**Remember**:

This book is **not** about the knowing the "right" thing to say. It's about saying the *real* thing in a way that keeps the door open, even when the moment feels like it's closing. Teaching isn't just what you assign. It's how you respond! Let this book help you *"Talk Like a Teacher"*, the one you were meant to be even when the stakes are high.

# I

# Pushback, Refusal, and Limits

*For when students push back, refuse, or test boundaries. Maybe you've heard, "This is stupid," or "You can't make me" in your classroom.*
*The responses in this section meet student resistance with calm and caring confidence instead of control that causes chaos.*

# "This is boring/I am bored."

**You say:**

"I get that because I feel that way sometimes too. But even the boring parts help your brain get stronger. Let's try to find something strange, crazy, or funny about what we're doing."

*** 

**Why it works:**

*Still validates the emotion. Builds trust by being human first, then optimistic about growth. Invites the student to engage with the material in their own way or a new way than is presented in the lesson.*

# "I don't get this."

**You say:**

"Thanks for letting me know. Let's figure out how to make it clear for you and what would help make it click. Can I start by explaining it step by step again?"

*\*\*\**

*Why it works:*

*Keeps the classroom emotionally safe by rewarding honesty, not punishing confusion. Shifts from blaming the student to problem-solving with the student. Offers a low-pressure, familiar entry point back into the learning.*

# "I already know this."

**You say:**

"Awesome, then your job is to prove it so well that I could hand your work to someone else and they'd understand it too. That's mastery!"

\* \* \*

**Why it works:**

*Acknowledges their confidence without letting them opt out. Shifts the task from doing to teaching, which deepens understanding. Keeps them engaged by raising the bar instead of lowering expectations.*

# "I don't want to."

**You say:**

"I get that. Want to start with just one step and see how it feels? Or maybe we can find a different way to do it, or even a better time? Let's figure this out together."

* * *

**Why it works:**

*Acknowledges the feeling while easing them in. Offers options as scaffolding. Becomes collaborative, never combative.*

# "You can't make me."

**You say:**

"I don't want to make you. I want to help you see what makes you to start by yourself. You matter in this class, and we need you in the game with us. When you're ready, I'll be here."

* * *

**Why it works:**

*Leans into relationship building instead of control and imbalance. Reminds the student they belong, even when they resist.*

# "I don't care."

**You say:**

"Maybe not right now. And that's OK. But I'll keep showing up until you do. I'll be here."

* * *

***Why it works:***

*Acknowledges the feeling/state and confirms there's nothing wrong with how the student feels. Models consistency and care.*

## "Why do we have to learn this?"

**You say:**

"That's probably the most important question, and I'm glad you asked. Let's take time to find out where this shows up in the real world and how YOU might see it sooner or later."

* * *

**Why it works:**

*Shares power, offers a new related option, and treats them like a curious autonomous thinker instead of a challenger.*

# "This is stupid."

**You say:**

"Let's find the parts that aren't. And maybe it is. But so is pineapple on pizza and that hasn't stopped anyone. Let's give it a try, I believe you can do this."

*** 

**Why it works:**

*Redirects energy toward curiosity instead of defense. Lightens the mood while keeping things moving. Powerful and grounded, holds both truth and expectations.*

# "I'm not doing this."

**You say:**

"Okay, want to check in privately in a minute? You deserve what you need to get through this. Whether you do it or not is your choice, but my job is to hold the door open."

*＊＊＊*

**Why it works:**

*Responds with calm curiosity, not confrontation. Subtly reframes the assignment as something they can do with the right tools. Prevents a power struggle and puts responsibility gently back in their hands. Expresses unconditional support without chasing them.*

# "Can I just do it later?/I'll do it later."

**You say:**

"You could. But now, you've got support, space, and focus, all rare things. Let's use that."

* * *

***Why it works:***

*Acknowledges their autonomy without being dismissive. Reframes the present moment as an opportunity, not a demand. Subtly appeals to logic and emotional maturity. Invites, rather than commands.*

# "I did it in my head."

**You say:**

"I believe you. Now show me the path your brain took — that's where the real learning lives."

\* \* \*

**_Why it works:_**

*Affirms their ability instead of doubting them. Teaches that explaining thinking is a skill, not just a requirement. Puts the focus on process over product, which supports long-term learning.*

# "Is this for a grade?"

**You say:**

"Sometimes. But right now, it's for your brain and that's the part that lasts longer than a number."

*** 

*Why it works:*

*Doesn't dodge the question, but shifts the focus to internal motivation. Emphasizes the value of learning for them, not just compliance. Builds a culture of thinking beyond points.*

# "Can I just guess?"

**You say:**

"You *can* guess but if you slow down and give it one honest try, you might surprise yourself. I'm more interested in your brain than your guess."

* * *

**Why it works:**

*Honors their autonomy while redirecting toward effort. Keeps the challenge low-pressure, emphasizing growth over perfection. Centers the student's thinking, not just the answer.*

# "Nobody else has to do this."

**You say:**
"That might be true but I'm not here to give everyone the same thing. I'm here to give *you* what you need to grow. And right now, this is part of that."

\* \* \*

*Why this works:*
*Avoids arguing the facts or getting defensive. Reinforces differentiated support in a clear, non-condescending way. Repositions the task as an investment in them, not a punishment. Ends with quiet authority and clarity, not threat or shame.*

# "Why are you calling on me?"

**You say:**

"Because I trust what you bring to the table and I want others to hear what you have to say."

* * *

**Why it works:**

*Affirms the student's value while acknowledging, instead of shutting down, their discomfort.*

# "I'm not good at this."

**You say:**

"I get that you feel like that right now but after we find your starting point, things can get clearer. Can I begin with you?"

*　*　*

**Why it works:**

*Shows empathy without agreement which is essential for gently challenging self-doubt. Uses "starting point" to imply everyone begins somewhere. Invites, rather than instructs, which gives agency back to the student.*

# "I give up."

**You say:**

"OK, let's sit and soak that in for a second, it's completely normal to get frustrated. When you're ready let's find out what your next move is."

*** 

**Why it works:**

*Respects the emotional moment instead of pushing through it. Normalizes struggling. Hands control back to the student. Centers action and a next step, not the feeling of failure.*

# "I'm done." (When they're not)

**You say:**

"Rest if you need to. I'm not giving up on you and I know you can finish this, just let me know when you're ready to start again."

\* \* \*

*Why it works:*

*Gives student choice in how they proceed with the material. Models persistence without pressure. States belief in student. Invites student to begin again at their own pace.*

# "I can't do this."

**You say:**

"That's ok you're feeling like that. I'll keep things open and ready for you when you're ready to step back in. No pressure."

*\*\*\**

***Why it works:***

*Removes shame or defensiveness by accepting, not correcting, their words. Keeps the academic task from becoming a source of threat or failure. Closes the loop with an invitation and emotional safety.*

# "I'm scared I'll mess up."

**You say:**

"If you mess up it means you were brave enough to try! Your effort is worth way more than your result, give it a go!"

*　*　*

*Why it works:*

*Redefines failure as a sign of courage, not weakness. Helps perfectionist or anxious students take that critical first step. Centers process over product, which is key for building grit and confidence. Warmly encourages action.*

## "I'm trying but I just don't get it."

**You say:**

"Trying is everything so keep that up, you're doing amazing. But for now let's slow down and look at this from another angle."

* * *

**Why it works:**

*Immediately affirms the student's effort, which is often the most fragile thing in the moment. Reminds them that struggle and progress can coexist. Shows you're adapting to their needs, not making them feel inadequate. Makes the next attempt feel fresh instead of like "failing again."*

# "I hate this class."

**You say:**

"You don't have to love this class, but I do care about making it better for you. Want to tell me what's not working and we can go from there?"

**If the student responds negatively, then say:**

"That's ok. I'll keep showing up for you."

\* \* \*

**Why it works:**

*Validates their feelings. Maintains authority while showing care. Gives a choice in the matter. Models consistency and unconditional support.*

## "I hate this school."

**You say:**

"It sounds like something here is making you really upset. Do you want to tell me what's been hard so we can figure out how to make it a little easier? Don't hold back from speaking your experience, I'm all ears."

\* \* \*

**Why it works:**

*Validates the student's emotional experience without taking it personally. Gently invites dialogue to get to the root cause without judgment.*

# "I hate you."

**You say:**

"It sounds like you are upset. I am not going to take that personally, but I do want to know what's going on underneath. I'll be here if you want to talk it out."

\* \* \*

*Why it works:*

*Acknowledges the student's emotional state without internalizing it and creating conflict. Invites further conversation to get to the cause of the emotion to improve the relationship, but leaves it up to the student. Models consistency in showing up.*

# "You do too much."

**You say:**

"It sounds like you're feeling overwhelmed or maybe annoyed with me. Want to help me understand what is too much right now?"

* * *

***Why it works:***

*Acknowledges how the student feels. Doesn't get defensive. Invites the student to clarify their needs, which often reduces resistance.*

# "You're not funny."

**You say:**

"Fair enough, different people find different things funny! But as long as joy belongs in here, I will keep trying my best."

*　*　*

***Why it works:***

Acknowledges criticism without bitterness, and gently insists on joy as part of classroom culture. Models persistence in optimism.

# "You never said that."

**You say:**

"Maybe I didn't say it clearly or maybe it got lost in the moment. Let's reset here and now so we are all on the same page. Always let me know if something doesn't match up. I'll try to be clearer next time!"

* * *

**Why it works:**

*Removes blame, models shared accountability, and keeps the tone light while course correcting.*

# "You aren't my mom/dad."

**You say:**

"No I am not. I am just someone who cares about you a lot."

*  *  *

**Why it works:**

*Confirms what the student says (unless the student is your child) without taking offense or making it personal. Restates unconditional care and acceptance of the student.*

# "You're a bad teacher."

**You say:**

"That hurts to hear, but I want to understand where it's coming from. I always want to reflect and improve, for real. Let's talk when you're ready."

*  *  *

**Why it works:**

*Regulates your own emotions. Models reflection and professional development. Defuses blame while inviting reflection and repair.*

## "This _____ is trash."

**You say:**
 "If that's how it feels, tell me why. I'm open to making things better for you."

* * *

**Why it works:**
 *Turns insult into opportunity for constructive dialogue.*

# "This is torture."

**You say:**

"I don't want it to feel that way. Let's scale it back a little and figure out where it got to be overwhelming."

* * *

***Why it works:***

*Responds to dramatization with calm care and concrete help.*

# "Leave me alone."

**You say:**

"Got it. I'll give you some space for now. I'm still here when you're ready. You don't have to go through it alone, even if it feels like that right now."

*  *  *

**Why it works:**

*Responds calmly without argument or escalation. Meets their immediate emotional need for distance. Reminds them that support hasn't been withdrawn. Addresses the deeper feeling often hidden under anger or shutdown: isolation.*

## "I don't even respect my mom."

**You say:**

"Sounds like trust or respect is really hard for you right now. You don't have to like me, but I'll always treat you with respect. And I'll be here when you're ready."

*** 

**Why it works:**

*Avoids punishment or power struggle. Models the very respect being questioned, while anchoring the adult's calm authority.*

# "Whatever."

**You say:**

"Sounds like you're done with the conversation. That's okay for now. Just know I'm still listening when we're ready to talk respectfully."

*＊ ＊ ＊*

***Why it works:***

*Names what's happening without sarcasm or judgment. Temporarily releases pressure, preventing escalation. Keeps the door open and communicates emotional safety.*

# "Shut up."

**You say:**

"I can hear you're upset. I'll listen once we can talk respectfully. For now let's take a moment and we'll try again."

*  *  *

**Why it works:**

*Maintains calm boundaries. Models self-regulation, giving the student space to deescalate while preserving teacher authority.*

# II

# Identity and Insecurity

*From "I'm ugly" to "I can't do this," these moments call for radical empathy. Reframe your students' self-doubts and show up when they need it most.*

# "I'm fat."

**You say:**

"You're noticing changes in your body, but it's important to be kind to yourself through all of them. I see someone who is kind, hardworking, and fun to be around which is really what stands out about you. Want to tell me more about how you're feeling or how I can support?"

* * *

**Why it works:**

*Acknowledges the student's perception. Opens space for body-positive dialogue and support, rather than dismissal or quick fixes. Offers a look at identity tied to more than body talk.*

# "I want to be skinny."

**You say:**

"It's okay to care about how you feel in your body but skinny doesn't mean better. Instead of skinny, what if the goal was strong, happy, and healthy, whatever that looks like for you? How do you really want to feel?"

\* \* \*

**Why it works:**

*Acknowledges without reinforcing harmful standards. Shifts the focus beyond physical appearance without shame.*

# "I'm ugly."

**You say:**

"I don't see that at all, I see someone with such a good heart that it shows on their face. We all have days where we don't like how we look, but how you *feel* about yourself is way more powerful."

*\* \* \**

**Why it works:**

*Validates the feeling in a personal, sincere way without agreeing or simply dismissing. Names the emotion and counters shame with empathy and positive self-perception.*

## "I don't like how I look."

**You say:**

"That's a tough feeling to carry. I'm here to remind you there's more to you than what the mirror shows. Do you want to talk about what's been bothering you with me or someone else you trust?"

*\*\*\**

**Why it works:**

*Offers emotional safety and a chance to talk without minimizing the feeling. Balances care with subtle redirection toward self-worth.*

# "I want plastic surgery one day."

**You say:**

"What I'm hearing is that there is something you're unhappy with about your appearance that you feel like you need to fix. Can we talk more about what's bothering you and also what you value about yourself?"

* * *

**Why it works:**

*Validates the feeling without judgment. Invites a deeper conversation and gently redirects toward self-worth.*

# "I'm gay."

**You say:**

"Thanks for sharing that with me. I see you, and you're safe with me exactly as you are. This is a safe space for all."

* * *

**Why it works:**

*Models unconditional affirmation and safety around identity.*

# "I'm trans."

**You say:**

"I appreciate you trusting me. If there's anything you want me to do like use a different name or pronouns just let me know."

\* \* \*

**Why it works:**

*Keeps the student in control of their own identity. Shows willingness to support and affirm student identity.*

# "I feel invisible."

**You say:**

"This class would not be the same without you. Let's figure out how to make sure you feel that too. I'm really glad you told me. You matter here and I see you, even if it hasn't felt that way. Please help me know how I can help you feel more seen or heard."

*  *  *

**Why it works:**

*Names their value and starts a plan. Meets the moment with presence and care.*

# "I wish I wasn't here."

**You say:**

"I'm really glad you are. And I'm going to help make this a place you actually want to be."

* * *

**Why it works:**

*Counters despair with presence and active care.*

# "I suck."

**You say:**

"Sounds like you're feeling really down on yourself. I see strengths in you. Want to talk about what's fueling this thought so we can challenge it together?"

* * *

**Why it works:**

*Mirrors the student's self-talk to show understanding. Reframes with observed strengths and collaborative problem-solving.*

# III

# Peer Drama and Conflict

*School can be a mess with friendship fallout, playground pettiness, and beyond.*
*This section helps you coach kids through conflict without taking sides, hurting feelings, or losing your mind.*

# "I don't want to be their friend anymore."

**You say:**

"Friendships change and that can be hard. You don't have to stay close, but let's keep things respectful between you. Let me know if you need any help or if you want me to check in."

*  *  *

**Why it works:**

*Affirms boundaries and the change. Models emotional maturity and peer respect. Opens a door to accountability/support in maintaining respectful boundaries.*

## "My classmate is so annoying."

**You say:**

"It's okay to feel frustrated with people. You can always stay kind. Think about what you can you do to stay focused and handle it without causing more stress for yourself. Do you want some help setting some boundaries while staying respectful?"

* * *

**Why it works:**

*Validates the feeling. Redirects power and control back to the student. Teaches social skills without excusing bad behavior.*

# "I'm not saying sorry."

**You say:**

"It's okay if you're not ready yet. Let me know when you feel like talking and we can work through it when you're ready."

*  *  *

**Why it works:**

*Deescalates power struggle. Honors emotional autonomy while keeping the door open for repair.*

# "Shut up." (to a peer)

**You say:**

"OK, I can see you're frustrated. Let's use words that solve this problem. What do you need *right now*?"

*  *  *

***Why it works:***

*Acknowledges emotion without shaming. Redirects toward problem-solving language, teaches regulation. Asks student to express needs with words.*

## "You just called him/her____"

**You say:**

"Thanks for speaking up. I want to be really clear I would never call someone _____. Can we talk about what you heard so I can clear it up?"

* * *

**Why it works:**

*Immediately denies harm without shame. Affirms the student's advocacy and opens respectful dialogue.*

## "They keep touching my hair."

**You say:**

"That is not OK, that's your body and nobody has the right to touch you without your consent. I'll start right away on making sure you stay respected and safe."

*  *  *

**Why it works:**

*Offers immediate, clear validation. Reinforces that consent applies to all forms of physical interaction, even those others try to brush off as "just curious" or "just playful." Shows the student that you're not just listening, you're taking responsibility as an adult.*

# "I am being bullied."

**You say:**

"Thank you for telling me. That takes guts. My job now is to protect your peace and make sure this doesn't keep happening. You're not doing this alone."

*  *  *

**Why it works:**

*Acknowledges the emotional risk and strength it takes to speak up about bullying. Centers the student's emotional wellbeing, not just rule enforcement. Communicates immediate action, not passive listening.*

# "I'm always in trouble."

**You say:**

"Then let's start building your new story right here and now. Every day is a fresh start with no shame."

*　*　*

***Why it works:***

*Flips the script: instead of focusing on their past behavior, it gives them agency over their next chapter. Shows that transformation doesn't require waiting for a new week, class, or year, it starts now. Tells the student: you are not being held hostage by yesterday. Explicitly removes the emotional weight that often keeps students stuck in a "bad kid" loop.*

# "Nobody wants to go with me."

**You say:**

"That hurts, and I'm sorry you're feeling left out. Remember you matter to this space. Let's figure out a way to help you feel more connected because you deserve to feel included."

*  *  *

**Why it works:**

*Names the pain of exclusion. Signals action without fixing everything immediately.*

## "I don't have anyone to sit with."

**You say:**
 "You've got me right now and I'll help you find someone kind to sit with next."

* * *

**Why it works:**
 *Provides instant safe space and a plan for connection.*

# "Nobody likes me."

**You say:**

"I'm really sorry it feels that way. That's such a heavy feeling. I like you and I've seen others who do too, even if it doesn't feel like it right now. Want to talk about what's been going on?"

*\*\*\**

**Why it works:**

*Validates the emotion without confirming the belief. Shows empathy without pity. Counters distorted thinking with gentle truth. Invites conversation without pressure.*

# IV

# Grief, Home, and Big Reveals

*When home isn't safe or something big breaks, students bring that pain to class. These responses help you stay steady, ready, and kind through their biggest stories.*

# "My mom/dad died."

**You say:**

"I'm so sorry. That's an enormous loss. I don't have perfect words, but I'm here to listen or just sit with you. We can step out together and figure out what feels right for today."

*  *  *

**Why it works:**

*Names the pain without platitudes. Admits limits to avoid false comfort. Offers immediate space and co regulation, then collaboration on next steps.*

# "My sibling died."

**You say:**

"Losing a sibling can feel like losing a part of yourself. Thank you for telling me. Let's find a quiet spot so you can share what you need. Then we can plan how school can feel more gentle right now."

* * *

**Why it works:**

*Recognizes the unique sibling bond. Invites the student to guide the pace, emphasizing agency and individualized school adjustments.*

# "My grandparent died."

**You say:**

"Grandparents hold special places in our hearts. I'm so sorry you're hurting. Would you like to talk about your favorite memory of them, or would just sitting quietly feel better for now?"

* * *

**Why it works:**

*Acknowledges relationship significance. Offers a concrete coping option while honoring the need for silence.*

# "My pet died."

**You say:**

"Losing a pet can feel like losing family. It's okay to be sad. If you want, we can make a little memory card or take a short break to breathe."

*  *  *

**Why it works:**

*Validates depth of grief often minimized by adults. Suggests a tangible ritual that promotes healthy mourning and emotional regulation.*

## "I'm being abused."

**You say:**

"Thank you for telling me. I believe you. You are not in trouble, and you are not alone. I'm going to make sure you get help."

*  *  *

**Why it works:**

*Opens with gratitude instead of panic or disbelief, which sets a safe emotional tone. Offers the most powerful sentence a student in crisis can hear ("I believe you"). Clarifies that disclosure doesn't lead to punishment. Communicates that action will be taken immediately and professionally. Doesn't overshare details or make promises you can't keep.*

# "Another student touched me inappropriately."

**You say:**

"Thank you for telling me. You did the right thing, and I take this very seriously. I'm going to make sure you're safe and get help right away. You are not alone in this."

* * *

**Why it works:**

*Acknowledges courage. Affirms action, not blame. Builds confidence in adult response. Starts a safety plan.*

# "An adult touched me inappropriately."

**You say:**

"Thank you for telling me. You were right to speak up. I'm going to make sure you're safe, and I'll report this right away so the right people can help. You are not in trouble, and you are not alone."

*  *  *

**Why it works:**

*Validates the student's decision to speak up. Reassures follow through. Focuses on protection instead of fear or drama. Calms fear and shame.*

# "My family doesn't like/want me."

**You say:**

"That sounds really painful. Would you share what's happening at home so we can figure out ways to help you feel supported?"

*  *  *

***Why it works:***

*Validates hurt. Signals willingness to listen and connect the student to resources without blaming the family.*

# "I want to run away."

**You say:**

"That tells me something really hard is going on. I'm not going to let you face it alone. You don't have to run. You can talk, and I'll walk through this with you."

\*\*\*

**Why it works:**

*Responds to the feeling under the statement, not just the words. Instantly gives them a sense of safety and presence. Positions the adult as someone who stays.*

# "My parents are getting a divorce."

**You say:**

"That's heavy news. However you're feeling whether it be confused, relieved, or upset is OK. I'm here to listen, and we can loop in the counselor so you have extra support."

\* \* \*

**Why it works:**

*Validates complex emotions without assuming one reaction. Offers concrete pathway to broader resources.*

## "My parent is going to jail."

**You say:**

I know that's a lot for you to think about and I'm really sorry you have to. But you don't have to go through this alone. I appreciate you letting me know what's going on, do you want to talk with someone you trust or step out with me for a minute?"

*　*　*

**Why it works:**

*Acknowledges gravity of the situation. Offers immediate support without prying.*

# "I'm moving."

**You say:**

"Big changes like moving can stir up a lot of emotions like excitement, worry, or even anger. What's on your mind about it, and how can we make the time you have left here feel steady?"

* * *

**Why it works:**

*Normalizes mixed emotions. Shifts focus to student voice and transitional support.*

# "I'm pregnant."

**You say:**

"Okay. That's big, and I'm glad you told me. I'm not here to judge, just to help you stay safe and figure out what you need. Have you told anyone else yet, or do you want help with that?"

*　*　*

**Why it works:**

*Keeps the tone calm but acknowledges the seriousness. Validates without minimizing or overreacting. Makes your role clear as protector and helper not moral authority. Gives the student space for next steps.*

# "I feel hopeless."

**You say:**

"Thank you for telling me. You matter to me so let's step aside right now and talk privately so we can find some hope together."

* * *

**Why it works:**

Expresses immediate care. Moves conversation to a safe, quieter space for deeper assessment and support.

# "I feel depressed."

**You say:**

"Thank you for telling me. That takes a lot of strength. You don't have to go through this alone. I'm going to make sure you get the support you deserve."

*  *  *

**Why it works:**

*Recognizes courage and begins with trust. Affirms the student as strong not broken. Reduces isolation. Makes a plan for next steps.*

# "I want to kill myself."

**You say:**

"I'm really glad you trusted me with this. Your safety is my first priority so let's go together right now to get you help."

\* \* \*

*Why it works:*

*Immediate safety move; no promises of confidentiality that can't be kept. Removes any delay, modeling calm urgency and ensuring mandated reporting.*

# V

# Authority and School

*"I hate this class," "You're mean," "That's not fair!"
Manage friction, feedback, and trust with responses that
model strength and openness.*

# "My parents say it's OK to hit back."

**You say:**

"I respect that your parents want you to feel protected, and I want the same thing for you here at school. Here, your safest move is always to step away, speak up, and let me or another adult handle it. That way you stay out of trouble, no one gets hurt, and we fix the problem together."

*  *  *

**Why it works:**

*Validates family belief without disrespecting it. Reinforces school expectations while reframing them as important safety measures not simple behavior management. Shifts the focus from punishment to support. Keeps the child from feeling stuck between home and school values.*

# "My mom said she's going to get you fired."

**You say:**
It seems like there's been some tension at home about class and school. Would you like to talk about what's going on so I can understand better?"

*　*　*

*Why it works:*
*Defuses the threat without defensiveness. Refocuses the conversation on student emotions, not adult conflict.*

# "Do you believe in God/Are you a Christian?"

**You say:**

"That's a really important question, but I try to keep my beliefs private so everyone feels safe to be themselves here."

* * *

***Why it works:***

*Addresses the student's curiosity. Models respectful boundary setting. Adheres to class values.*

# "You're picking on me."

**You say:**

"I'm sorry I'm making you feel that way, I get why it might feel like that. My job is to help you grow, not to make you feel small. If something I did felt unfair, I'm open to hearing about it after class."

\* \* \*

**Why it works:**

*Confirms that perception matters, regardless of intention. Helps the student reconnect with the idea that correction and accountability are part of growth. Teaches emotional regulation: not everything has to be solved in the heat of the moment.*

## "You're mean."

**You say:**

"I think being mean would be walking away from you and letting you just fail at this. I'm still here and will keep showing up for you."

\* \* \*

**Why it works:**

*Shifts the student's understanding of care from what feels good to what builds growth. Shows the student that you're not giving up, even if they're resisting. Models the kind of stability that many students are silently testing for when they lash out.*

# "You're racist."

**You say:**

"That's a serious thing to say, and I want to understand what made you feel that way. If I said or did something that came across that way, I want to hear it and learn. This classroom has to feel safe for you."

\* \* \*

**Why it works:**

*Models growth mindset, not fragility. Creates space for truth, not defensiveness.*

## "I don't trust teachers."

**You say:**

"You don't have to. Trust is something I earn, not expect. I'll be here either way."

*  *  *

**Why it works:**

*Removes pressure and invites trust through time and proof.*

# "That's not how another teacher does it."

**You say:**

"That totally makes sense! Every teacher has their own system. Anytime you want I can explain my system so you always know what to expect."

*　*　*

**Why it works:**

*Disarms the implied complaint by showing openness instead of opposition. Normalizes difference and sets the expectation that variation is part of school. Makes your expectations feel accessible and open to discussion, not hidden or rigid. Positions you as consistent and student-centered, even when your approach differs from others.*

# "I hate (other teacher)."

**You say:**

"You're clearly upset with [_____]. You can tell me what happened so we can address it respectfully and you can feel safe and heard. If something went wrong between you and them, maybe we can find a way to speak up or solve it without turning it into hate."

*＊ ＊ ＊*

**Why it works:**

*Acknowledges emotion without endorsing disrespect. Opens a restorative path rather than gossip or escalation.*

# "Can I stay in your room this period?"

**You say:**

"I appreciate that you feel safe here. I need to stick to the schedule, but let's plan a time when you can check in again here if you need to."

*  *  *

***Why it works:***

*Honors the underlying need for connection or escape. Maintains structure without rejecting the student.*

# "Can I eat lunch with you?" (And you have to say 'no')

**You say:**

"That means a lot that you asked! I need this little break to get things done, but I hope we can catch up again another time during the day."

* * *

**Why it works:**

*Affirms the bond. Models healthy boundaries without guilt or coldness.*

# "Why do we have to write an essay?"

**You say:**
 "Fair question. Writing an essay isn't about the essay, it's about learning how to organize your thoughts, back them up, and make people listen. That's a skill you'll use in almost anything, even outside school."

*　*　*

***Why it works:***
 *Opens a conversation, not a power struggle. Gets to the real 'why' with a surprising truth. Breaks down an essay into real, useful skills. Connects to life beyond the classroom. Gives relevance without exaggeration.*

## "I'm not a good test taker."

**You say:**

"A lot of smart people feel that way. Let's figure out how you can show what you know in a way that works better for you."

**Or, if in reference to standardized testing, say:**

"I hear you and this test doesn't come close to showing everything you're good at. But let's give it your best so you walk out knowing you didn't let fear make the choices. That test doesn't define you, your effort does."

* * *

**Why it works:**

*Normalizes the challenge. Shifts the conversation to strengths and support, not fixed identity. Reframes the test as incomplete or lacking instead of the student.*

# "This is too much work!"

**You say:**

"You don't have to finish it all at once. Let's take it one small piece at a time. How do you want to start?"

*＊＊＊*

***Why it works:***

*Shows the student they're not being rushed or expected to conquer it all in one sitting. Creates a collaborative tone. Flips the emotional switch from I'm trapped to I'm choosing.*

# "I'm not good at (subject)."

**You say:**

"A lot of people feel that way, even I feel that way sometimes! But keep in mind that feeling stuck is NOT the same as being bad at something. Let's see what a good starting point is for you and what you want to get better at. Just let me know when you're ready."

*\*\*\**

***Why it works:***

*Helps students understand that discomfort is common, not a personal failure. Gives the student language to challenge their own negative self-talk. Shifts the focus from what they can't do to what they can build from. Offers space and autonomy without pressure.*

# "I hate reading." (If they cannot read)

**You say:**

"I know reading can feel frustrating when it's hard. You're not alone and we can work on it together, one step at a time."

* * *

**Why it works:**

Speaks to the root issue (struggle, not preference). Builds trust through non judgment and partnership.

# "I hate reading." (If they can read)

The truth is, this one is tough and I hear this a lot from kids who can read. I turn it into the same little dialogue that usually just ends with them trying to figure out what I said, but I do hope it sticks with them:

**"I hate reading"**
**"What, like you hate being *able* to read?"**
**"What? No. I hate like *reading*..."**
**"OH. See when I hear that**, I hear 'I hate reading like I hate seeing, smelling, touching, or tasting.' Reading to me is not something to really be loved or hated, it is just something we can do as humans. Getting good at reading is one of the most important and helpful things you can do for your life no matter who you are or what you do. Do you mean you hate reading *boring things*? Because I do too! I think everybody does. But don't let boring things stop you from getting better at reading. Let's find what YOU like to read today. Are you ready?"

**How do you respond to a student who says this?**

# "Can I just use the internet?"

**You say:**

"Absolutely, but first tell me what you think! Then when you look it up, tell me if you still think the same."

* * *

**Why it works:**

*Encourages personal thinking before digital help. Then encourages critical thinking engaged with what is found online.*

# "I don't want to say the Pledge of Allegiance."

**You say:**

"It's okay to think differently about these things. Part of what we're pledging is the freedom to choose."

*** 

*Why it works:*

*Acknowledges the student's wishes. Uses the moment to teach civic values.*

## "I wasn't listening/I didn't hear you."

**You say:**

"Thank you for being honest! Let's get you caught up."

*\*\*\**

**Why it works:**

*Shows appreciation for the student's honesty. Attempts to orient the student without blaming or shaming for not listening. Moves on with the class material instead of harping on bad habits.*

# "I don't have a pencil."

**You say:**
"No worries, I've got extras. Just grab one and get started. This is a good reminder to come prepared to class."

**NOTE:**
*ALWAYS take a student asking for a pencil as a sign of getting ready to start work.*

\* \* \*

**Why it works:**
*Keeps things moving, avoids shaming, but still sets an expectation.*

# "That's not fair." (Social)

**You say:**

"I get that it feels unfair and I'm open to hearing your side. But based on what I saw, this is our next step for now. We will definitely talk more if you want when things are calm."

*  *  *

**Why it works:**

*Acknowledges fairness as emotional, not just logical. Keeps the door open without inviting a blowup in front of others.*

# "That's not fair." (Academic)

**You say:**

"I hear you. Fair can feel really different depending on your point of view. I try to give everyone what they need but this is not always the exact same thing. If something's really bugging you, let's talk about it after class."

*  *  *

**Why it works:**

Prevents escalation by showing you're listening, not dismissing. Helps students understand that fairness is not always sameness. Clearly states your classroom philosophy in student-friendly terms while modeling equity in action. Provides a respectful outlet without derailing the moment.

# "Why did I get a (grade)?

**You say:**

"Let's look at your work together. I can show you how I got there, and we can figure out what our next step is."

* * *

**Why it works:**

*Shifts the conversation from judgment to growth. Offers transparency and hope.*

# "What can I do to improve my grade?"

**You say:**

"I really respect you for asking! Let's look at what's possible regarding your grade and either way, we'll come up with a plan so this class feels more doable moving forward."

* * *

**Why it works:**

*Validates effort. Balances accountability with encouragement and focus on the future.*

# "I don't want/need to graduate."

**You say:**

"That's a big statement. It seems like you feel graduation is unnecessary or out of reach…can you tell me what's making you feel this way about graduation right now?"

\* \* \*

**Why it works:**

*Avoids shaming or correcting. Opens a reflective conversation that might reveal hopelessness, pressure, or fear underneath the statement.*

## "This doesn't matter to me."

**You say:**

"That's real. Let's find a way to connect it to something that *does* matter to you."

*  *  *

**Why it works:**

Uses real instead of "okay" or "I understand," which hits deeper and signals respect for their perspective. Makes the next step collaborative, not forced. Opens the door to relevance, not by changing the assignment, but by helping them find themselves in it. Keeps the academic goal alive while respecting student voice.

# "School is pointless."

**You say:**

"School is a great place for you to become who you want to be, not a place to memorize numbers and letters and facts. Let's work together starting now to make this a place you feel matters."

* * *

**Why it works:**

*Reframes school as a launchpad for identity instead of a grind for grades. Humanizes the learning process and separates it from robotic task completion. Turns the teacher into a partner, not a taskmaster. Focuses not just on the content, but on the experience.*

# "What's the point?"

**You say:**

"I get that this might seem pointless, but remember the point is always YOU. You matter here and if something is feeling off, let's talk about it so you can have the best experience possible. The work is just a mirror."

\* \* \*

**Why it works:**

*Acknowledges that not everything feels meaningful all the time, a truth even adults relate to. Reminds the student that their growth, well-being, and self-discovery are central not the assignment. Suggests that schoolwork reflects effort, mindset, and growth. Reframes tasks as tools for self-awareness, not just hoops to jump through.*

# VI

# Body Needs and Embarrassing Moments

*Periods, poop, puke, and hunger, this section is about meeting human needs with quiet dignity, so no child ever feels humiliated for being a person.*

# "I'm having a bad morning/day."

**You say:**

"Thank you for showing up anyway. Please let me know anything I can do to help."

*  *  *

**Why it works:**

*Recognizes effort despite adversity. Opens up a line of support from you.*

# "I'm (too) tired."

**You say:**

"I believe you! Let's figure out what you can do today even if it's a little. Small, slow steps still count as progress."

* * *

*Why it works:*

*Counters a common fear: "They'll think I'm making excuses." Shifts the focus from what's impossible to what's possible. Encourages agency without pushing too hard. Reinforces that forward movement doesn't have to be dramatic to be meaningful.*

# "I'm hungry/Do you have food?"

**If you *can* offer food, say:**

"I've got something small you can eat, here you go. Let me know if this keeps happening so we can get you more support."

**If You *Can't* Offer Food (Policy or Supply), say:**

"I really wish I could give you something right now, but I can't. Want me to help you talk to the nurse or someone else who can help?

**For a gentle redirect with no mention of food, say:**

"I hear you. Let's get through this part of class, and I'll help you check in after because I don't want you staying hungry."

*\* \* \**

**Why it works:**

*Care now, solutions later. Maintains empathy with action. Acknowledges the need while keeping the class on track.*

# "I'm sleepy (after lunch)."

**You say:**

"Totally normal after lunch. Let's do something that helps you stay alert. Do you want to stretch, get a drink of water, or take the first part slow? You let me know how we can get your energy level back to normal."

\* \* \*

**Why it works:**

*Normalizes a biological rhythm. Offers regulated strategies that keep learning accessible. Gives the student the opportunity to self-adjust their own way.*

## "My classmate smells bad."

**You say:**
"Thank you for letting me know, I will handle it gently. If you're distracted, let's find a solution that doesn't hurt anyone."

* * *

**Why it works:**
*Protects dignity. Redirects to empathy and classroom values.*

# "I have to throw up."

**You say:**

"OK, let's get you to a bathroom right now. I'll walk with you. You're safe."

* * *

**Why it works:**

Signals control, not panic which reassures the student immediately. Communicates clear priority: your needs come first. Shows presence and care, even in an uncomfortable or embarrassing moment.

# "I just threw up."

**You say:**

"I'm sorry you're sick. Let's get you cleaned up and over to the nurse so you can rest."

* * *

***Why it works:***

*Shows empathy. Quickly shifts to practical care and minimizes embarrassment.*

## "I just peed/soiled myself."

**You say:**

"Thanks for telling me, that was really brave. You're not in trouble. Let's get you cleaned up and taken care of as quietly as possible. I've got your back."

*　*　*

**Why it works:**

*Shows empathy. Quickly shifts to practical care and minimizes embarrassment.*

# "I just started my period."

**You say:**

"Got it, do you want to head to the bathroom, the nurse or need anything from me?"

* * *

**Why it works:**

*Simple, calm, and gives student agency without making it a moment.*

# "Everyone's staring at me."

**You say:**

"I'll handle the crowd. You just focus on taking care of yourself. We've all had moments like this — I've got your back."

* * *

**Why it works:**

*Shows you're proactively protecting them from further embarrassment or attention. Reduces shame by shifting the focus from public perception to self-care. Builds trust and connection, especially when a student feels exposed.*

# VII

# Restoration, Repair, and Trust-Building

*After the blowup, the silence, and the eye roll is where the real healing begins.*
*Try these practical phrases to rebuild connection when trust feels cracked.*

# "I'm sorry."

**You say:**

"Thanks for saying that. I appreciate your words a lot. Are you okay if we talk about what led up to this too?"

* * *

***Why it works:***

*Accepts apology graciously. Leaves room for growth without turning it into a lecture.*

# "I love you."

**You say:**

"It is very kind for you to say that and I hope you know you matter to me and to this class."

*  *  *

***Why it works:***

*Acknowledges the vulnerability behind the statement without making it awkward or inappropriate. Frames their words as thoughtful and valid, without escalating emotional intensity. Reaffirms the teacher's care in a healthy, professional, and emotionally safe way. Provides emotional grounding without confusing roles or boundaries. Reinforces that the student is a valuable part of a community, not just in a one-on-one dynamic.*

# "You're my favorite teacher."

**You say:**

"That means a lot, thank you so much. I'm glad you feel so comfortable here, and I hope you always show up as your best self."

* * *

***Why it works:***

*Accepts the praise warmly. Gently centers student growth, not teacher favoritism.*

# "Why do you keep trying with me?"

**You say:**

"Because you're worth trying for. Even on the hard days, I still believe in you."

* * *

*Why it works:*

*Interrupts narratives of worthlessness with quiet, durable belief.*

# VIII

## Pocket Phrases

*These "pocket phrases" are fast, firm, and full of heart. These are your one-liners, resets, and power phrases to keep in your pocket for when you need to respond right now and keep things grounded.*

# When a student gets off topic

**You say:**

"That's definitely a brain saver for later, but right now, we're locked in on this. Stay with me."

\* \* \*

***Why it works:***

*Redirects with respect. Signals the student's curiosity is not wrong but mistimed. Clearly shifts the focus back.*

# When an inappropriate sexual topic comes up

**You say:**
 "That topic isn't appropriate for class. Let's pause the conversation. If you have genuine questions about it, we can talk privately or connect you with our nurse/counselor."

*** 

**Why it works:**
 *Sets a clear boundary without shaming. Provides a safe, private avenue for legitimate questions, preventing misinformation.*

# When a slur is used

**You say:**

"We don't use that word here because it hurts people. Take a breath. Let's talk about what led you to say it and how to repair the harm."

*** 

**Why it works:**

*Immediately stops the harm and names its impact. Couples accountability with an invitation to restorative dialogue, modeling an inclusive culture.*

# When a student is crying (uncontrollably)

**You say:**

"You don't have to explain anything right now. I've got you. Let's just breathe together until it doesn't feel this big."

* * *

*Why it works:*

*Removes pressure instead of adding to it. Anchors support and coregulates without minimizing, downplaying, or being artificial.*

# When you want to shut down a behavior gently

**You say:**

"I care about you too much to let that slide, let's reset."

*  *  *

**Why it works:**

Leads with care not control. Reframes correction as an act of respect and belief in what the student can do.

# When you remind them of your expectations

**You say:**

"I hold you to this standard because I believe in you. That hasn't changed."

*  *  *

**Why it works:**

*Reinforces expectations without threats, guilt, or lectures. out threats, guilt, or lectures. Shifts the focus from compliance to respect for the student.*

# When you want to acknowledge effort

**You say:**

"That wasn't easy, and you still showed up. I see that and I hope you do too."

*  *  *

***Why it works:***

*Honors the student's effort without exaggeration. Names the difficulty and recognizes the success in showing up.*

# When you need to pause to gather yourself

**You say:**
 "Give me a second. I want to respond, not react."

\* \* \*

**Why it works:**
 *Demonstrates the human nature of needing to pause to collect oneself. Names the intention to respond to the student in a constructive way.*

## When you want to calm a tense moment:

**You say:**

"Let's both take some even breaths. I want this to go well for you."

** * **

**Why it works:**

*Immediately creates an environment of support. Invites the student to join in a proven meditative practice. Encourages thinking ahead of the moment.*

# When you want to redirect without power struggle:

**You say:**
"This matters, and so do you. Let's figure it out together."

*＊ ＊ ＊*

***Why it works:***
Centers both the task and the student. Invites collaboration.

# When you want to connect after conflict:

**You say:**

"We had a rough moment and we can still move forward. I'm glad you're here."

*  *  *

**Why it works:**

*Acknowledges the conflict without dwelling on it. Doesn't accuse. Signals repair is possible. Reminds the student they still belong.*

# When you want to encourage a fresh start

**You say:**
"New moment. New choice. Let's try again."

* * *

**Why it works:**
*Breaks the cycle of shame. Reminds the student every moment is a chance to start fresh.*

# IX

# Student Archetypes

*Not every student needs the same words. In this section, you'll meet ten common student types like the Shutdown Teenager, the Class Clown, and the Screen Team. Learn how to respond in a way that reaches them. Each archetype comes with a snapshot of behaviors, a tailored approach for each type, and key phrases that build connection, defuse tension, and meet the moment with empathy and clarity. Know each type and choose the tone to respond the real way.*

# The Little Dynamo

**Snapshot:** Constant motion, blurts answers, struggles to wait turns.

**Approach:** Mirror their enthusiasm, set clear micro-goals, give a physical outlet.

**Key phrase:**

"Let's park the rocket fuel in your body. Show me 'quiet hands' for ten seconds, then we high five."

# The Sensitive Soul

**Snapshot:** Tears easily, takes criticism to heart, worries about fairness.

**Approach:** Warm tone, name the feeling, offer a concrete next step.

**Key phrase:**
"I can see that hurt. You're safe, and we can fix it together. First, take one slow breath with me."

# The Big Feelings/Small Kid

**Snapshot:** Quick to anger, may shout "That's not fair," slams materials.

**Approach:** Stay neutral, give language for the feeling, offer two choices.

**Key phrase:**

"Sounds like you're frustrated. You can cool off at the calm corner or talk it out with me. Which helps you right now?"

# The Anxious Test-Taker

**Snapshot:** Hands shake before assessments, negative self-talk, blanking out.

**Approach:** Shrink the moment, focus on effort over outcome, anchor with a ritual.

**Key phrase:**
"This page is just six questions. Tackle one, then lift your pencil and stretch. Effort first, grade second."

# The Class Clown

**Snapshot:** Craves laughs, derails lessons, hides insecurity in jokes.

**Approach:** Acknowledge wit, redirect spotlight to purposeful role.

**Key phrase:**

"You've got real comic timing. Use it to help us review the vocab—give us a funny sentence for each word."

# The Quiet Observer

**Snapshot:** Rarely speaks, eyes always tracking, grades solid but connection thin.

**Approach:** Low-stakes invitations, private praise, patience with silence.

**Key phrase:**
"I notice you catch details others miss. If you're up for it, share one observation when you feel ready."

# The Perfectionist

**Snapshot:** Erases holes in paper, cries over a 92 percent, procrastinates from fear.

**Approach:** Celebrate risk taking, model mistake-making, set "good enough" checkpoints.

**Key phrase:**
"Goal for today, an imperfect draft. Perfect comes later. Right now messy progress wins."

# The Screen Teen

**Snapshot:** Phone always out, gaming references, struggles to sustain offline focus.

**Approach:** Connect content to digital interests, use timed tech breaks, clarify non negotiables.

**Key phrase:**
"I'll give a two minute scroll at the halfway mark. Until then, phones face down and we speed run this task like a level."

# The Activist

**Snapshot:** Challenges rules, passionate about causes, quick to call out "unfair."

**Approach:** Validate purpose, channel critique into constructive action, keep dialogue open.

**Key phrase:**

"I hear your point about fairness. Let's map three concrete changes you'd propose and who needs to hear them. Your voice matters most when it turns into a plan."

# The Shut Down Student

**Snapshot:** Head down, monosyllables, "whatever."

**Approach:** Go low-pressure, name heaviness, offer presence without demand.

**Key phrase:**
 "I don't know everything you're carrying. You don't have to talk now, just know I'm not letting go of you."

# X

# Grade-Specific Responses

*Because a kindergartner and a high schooler need different kinds of love. Grade level tweaks to keep your responses real, relevant, and age appropriate.*

# Kindergarten

**"You don't have to know how yet, that's what school is for."**
*Teaches patience with learning and builds safety for risk-taking.*

**"Let's practice being brave, not perfect."**
*Helps with separation anxiety, mistakes, and trying new things.*

**"Your job is to try and my job is to help."**
*Establishes roles and creates a secure sense of partnership.*

# First Grade

**"It's okay to not understand it yet, we're learning, not racing."**
*Counters comparison and builds a growth mindset.*

**"When your brain struggles, that means it's growing."**
*Turns frustration into evidence of progress.*

**"You are not behind, you're on your own learning path."**
*Protects confidence and keeps focus on personal growth.*

## Second Grade

**"You don't need to be perfect, you just need to practice."**
*Sets healthy expectations for effort and revision.*

**"Let's talk to ourselves like we'd talk to a friend."**
*Introduces emotional regulation and self-talk tools.*

**"Just because it's hard doesn't mean you can't do it."**
*Builds persistence and counters negative self-talk.*

# Third Grade

**"Show me the clue (in the story) that proves your answer."**
*Signals the jump from 'reading the words' to 'using evidence.'*

**"Multiplication is turbo charged adding so let's fire up the engine."**
*Turns a new, abstract skill into an exciting upgrade.*

**"Fair doesn't always mean equal. Can you tell me what *you* need, not what your neighbor has."**
*Tackles the emerging fairness debates of eight year olds.*

# Fourth Grade

**"Your writing is your megaphone so make me hear it from the hallway!"**
*Pushes expanding vocab and voice in opinion pieces.*

**"Decimals only look scary but if we just zoom in: one step, one tenth, one hundredth..."**
*Breaks down a famously intimidating new concept.*

**"Real scientists change the plan when the data says something different. What will you change?"**
*Fits perfectly with inquiry projects and first true lab reports.*

# Fifth Grade

**"Middle school will thank you for everything you organize today."**
*Links current work to looming independence.*

**"Complex problems are just Lego blocks. Snap them apart, solve, and click them back together."**
*Demystifies multi step math and long form tasks.*

**"Leaders ask sharper questions so what's one only *you* can bring to this lesson?"**
*Invites higher-level thinking and positions them as role models.*

## Sixth Grade

**"Your brain's in upgrade mode that's why things feel messy. Messy is progress."**
*Normalizes growing pains with a confident reframe.*

**"Middle school is where habits get loud so make sure yours are saying something good."**
*Connects behavior to identity in a way they've never thought about.*

**"You don't have to *love* the assignment but you can *own* it."**
*Acknowledges resistance while maintaining standards.*

# Seventh Grade

**"You're not hard to teach, you're just starting to ask harder questions. That's a good thing!"**
*Transforms defiance into maturity and honors curiosity.*

**"This isn't only about school it's also about practicing how to think when things feel boring or pointless."**
*Takes on the "why does this matter?" spiral head on.*

**"You control the volume of your voice in this room, not with how loud you are, but how you affect others."**
*Elevates communication skills without lecturing.*

# Eighth Grade

**"High school won't ask if you're ready, it just starts. This is your warm up lap."**

*Links present effort to near future stakes.*

**"This project is your chance to stop repeating answers and start creating your own real arguments."**

*Challenges students to step into deeper academic identity.*

**"How you show up *today* is how people will remember you. What story are you writing?"**

*Taps into legacy, self concept, and emotional awareness.*

# Ninth Grade

**"High school isn't harder, it's just louder. Let's quiet the noise and focus in."**
*Reframes overwhelm as manageable and within their control.*

**"Your transcript started yesterday, what do you want it to say about you next year?"**
*Makes abstract longterm thinking immediate and personal.*

**"The skill isn't knowing the answer, it's knowing how to keep going when you don't."**
*Develops grit without shame.*

# Tenth Grade

**"This is the year people stop reminding you about stuff, but colleges still watch. Who are you when no one's checking in?"**
*Confronts motivation dropoff with identity-based challenge.*

**"If this feels boring, you're actually ready to go deeper not give up."**
*Redirects disengagement into ownership and curiosity.*

**"You don't need a crazy complicated plan, just 10 focused minutes. Start there."**
*Shrinks overwhelm and encourages momentum.*

# Eleventh Grade

**"Grades matter, but so do sleep, sanity, and knowing your own limits. Burnout isn't worth a good grade."**
*Protects students from perfectionism and collapse.*

**"You don't have to know your future but you do need to take that version of you seriously."**
*Validates uncertainty while demanding presence.*

**"You can't control every door but you *can* hold the key."**
*Empowers students facing college/career unknowns.*

# Twelfth Grade

**"People will stop giving you rubrics and checklists soon. That's why these matter now."**
*Prepares students for self direction in life and work.*

**"What you turn in today is a piece of your reputation tomorrow."**
*Connects academic choices to real world perception.*

**"There's no bell in real life. You have to know when it's time to move on."**
*Signals maturity, transition, and readiness.*

# XI

# Power Phrases

*These short "power phrases" pack a punch and teachers should be saying them every day, throughout the day. Repeating these phrases intentionally builds connection, classroom culture, and confidence in students and teachers alike. Give them a try today.*

# List

"You matter here, everyday."
 "You're doing amazing."
 "You did it."
 "That was kind."
 "You got this."
 "Tell me more."
 "Keep going."
 "You're almost there."
 "You worked hard."
 "Nice self control."
 "That took courage."
 "Thanks for trying."
 "Let's try again."
 "I'm glad you're here."
 "I hear you."
 "That's a win."
 "You bounced back."
 "Proud of you."
 "That's leadership."
 "Such good thinking!"
 "You improved today by_____."
 "Good question."

"I noticed that."
"Way to focus."
"You stayed calm."
"That's progress."
"I'll be here."

Add your own below!

# XII

# Final words and Acknowledgments

# Talk Like a Teacher

## Final Words

No one can 'Talk Like a Teacher' on their first day. It's something you pick up in pieces. In between the bells, in chaos, in quiet, and sometimes right in the middle of a crisis, this book is here to remind you that every moment is a chance to **respond, not react**. To protect your peace while protecting theirs. To lead without power trips. To talk like a teacher. Not a robot, not a savior, not a doormat. Just a real, thoughtful human who knows how much words matter and more importantly, how much their students matter.

**Keep using this book. Keep adapting it. Make it your own. And above all, keep showing up for yourself and your students!**

## Acknowledgments

To the teachers who never lost their voice, thank you for showing us it's possible.
To the teachers who *did* lose it but came back stronger, this book is for you.
To the students who tested us, trusted us, and sometimes taught us more

than we taught them, your words built this book.
And to every educator flipping through this during lunch, after school, or in a crisis, I see you!

# About the Author

Chase has been a teacher for over 10 years.
He's heard a lot and can't wait to hear more.

www.ingramcontent.com/pod-product-compliance
Lightning Source LLC
Chambersburg PA
CBHW041040050426
42337CB00059B/5078